MW01482211

Shine On!

SHINY BITS OF WISDOM

Published in the United States by Create Space, a division of Amazon, Inc.
Library of Congress Catagloging-in-Publication data
Herbert, Cathy and Vredenburg, DandeLyon
ISBN-13: 978-1499716764 ISBN-10:1499716761
Design by Naina Lal

You are more amazing and wonderful than you think.
Believe in yourself, be kind, and shine on!
Look for the beauty in the world, smile when you see it,
and remember that
this life is yours to enjoy.
Today will be a new day. Put aside your worries and fears.
Shine like the bright star you are.
Your beauty is unique, formed by your rough edges as well as your smooth ones. In the end,
know that you are perfect, and perfectly shiny.

Soon, I will have long legs, a strong heart, and powerful lungs.

I will breathe deeply and run for miles, just for fun.

But for now, I will stay close to home, with you.

Always know that you are the reflection of all that is good in the universe.

Reflect on how special you are...and shine.

Everything that you contribute to your world is unique,

gifts that only you can give.

Shine on!

Thank you to everyone that I love (and have loved) in my life.
Love speaks a quiet language.
Shine on!
Stand close together in the sunlight
with someone you love,
look forward to all your tomorrows,
and revel in the beauty that surrounds you
on this—and every—day.
Find the beauty in yourself. It's there.

Softly whispered, remembered always, tiny moments make love special.
I see by the gentleness in your eye that you will become my true friend, and that
I will treasure you for all time.
Enjoy the magic moments in your special life.
Look for the warmth, love, and laughter
that surround you.
Allow yourself to shine.
You deserve it.

When you come downstairs, barefoot in the early morning cold,
think about the warmth of the day to come.
Even when you shiver, feel a hint of the warmth from the future that will be yours—
when you let yourself shine.
The beauty of the world is all around us,
in everything from the soft sheen of a horse's coat to the
patterns of light reflected on ice.
Take a minute, see it, and shine on!
I will sparkle and shine in the sun and focus on all that is good in my life—
those I love and who love me.

Shine like the bright star you are!

Soon, it'll be a great new day...if you allow it to be that way.

Yes! Your day will be wonderful.

Live it, love it, shout out loud about it.

It's yours.

The joy of movement, the thrill of being:

To see this is to understand all that is magical in the world.

After the winter storm, the sun will shine again and

YOUR day will be full of warmth

and beauty—a gift to be treasured.

When the air is still, listen for the soft sounds of love that surround you,
under the chatter of everyday life.
Look for the beauty and joy that fill the world
but that often pass, unnoticed.
Watch, listen, and marvel.
Kindness will fill your world—if you let it.
Take a minute to shine today.
Your world is waiting for you.
Treasure those moments yet to come.

Enjoy your beautiful life. Yes, you deserve it.
And it belongs to you.
Run to meet the future, so full of all good things.
Welcome the day with those you love
and who love you.
Take the time to appreciate all that is beautiful
in the life you have.
Set aside a moment to play—and shine—today.

Words have power. Talk to yourself with kind words,
because YOU are listening.
Take a deep breath, relax,
and make your life spectacular!
In your life, on this day,
the choices before you offer endless possibilities.
Make each choice count.
Be creative, make a change, take a walk, be kind.
Gather up all your wonderful opportunities and
live your bright and shiny life like you mean it!

Sometimes you just have to veer off in a new direction
to find the magic in your life.
Even though your eyes are on the future,
keep your heart close to home, always.
We may choose different paths, but, at the end of the day,
we will be together, safe and warm.
You are the architect, builder, subcontractor, and interior designer of your life.
Make your life strong and beautiful,
filled with joy and love.

Hello, World!
Even when I am old, I will remember how it feels to
look at the world with wonder.
On this bright new morning,
put aside all the doubts and fears;
they belong to yesterday—
and appreciate all the possibilities of the great new day that is today.
Show the world how you shine
in everything you do.

What a wonderful life.
Love it, love yourself, and look with wonder at the world around you.
Try hard, be kind, and smile when you can.
Know that YOU are spectacular.
Today offers so many opportunities for a smile, a laugh, a new beginning.
Make the most of today—every day!
Find the beauty in the truth about who you are and celebrate it:
You were born to be amazingly shiny!

Find the amazing beauty in your quiet strength.
Discover the amazing grace in your quiet strength.
Know that your soul is amazing, graceful, and strong.
Learn these lessons, and you will be free. Peace.
The world is full of magic, and you make it happen.
You are right on time with the universe!
Be present in the now to see your way to your future.
The signs that will guide you already surround you;
open your heart and you will see them clearly.

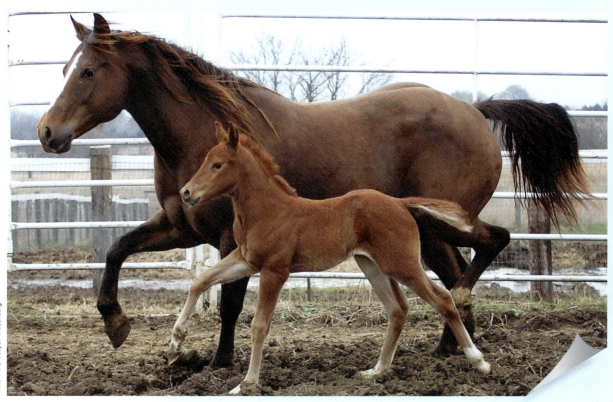

Shine like the bright star you are!
On this day, be present
in all the special moments of your life.
Start small, smell your coffee, savor the aroma,
and explore the experience.
Allow the ordinary to become extraordinary—
because you are amazingly shiny.
See all the beauty in the truth of who you are.
When you do, celebrate YOU! And know this:
You were born to shine.

Love softly, love well.

Always remember love's warmth. When you do, smile.

In that moment, you will shine.

Moments of closeness, moments of love.

Always remember how special they are.

A soft touch, a gentle sound. These make all the world seem new and magical.

Give kindness every day, and, in every moment,

appreciate what you have.

We will break each other's hearts too many times to count

but still face the day together....always.

A smile is a message from your soul to the world.
We are all beautifully imperfect, and that makes us human.
We are each unique, in both our beauty and our flaws.
Give yourself permission to strive for progress
without demanding perfection—from yourself or others.
Celebrate this day, honor yourself,
and enjoy the process of living.
Whatever this day brings,
know that you are unlike any other being in the universe.

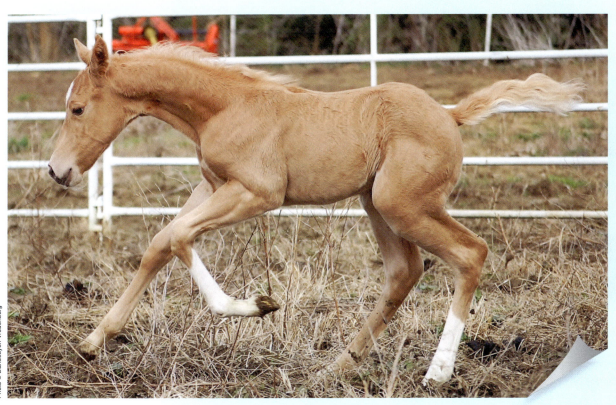

Radiate kindness and it will be reflected back at you.
Shine on!
Take a break from your crazy life and
notice the quiet beauty that surrounds you.
The obstacles you face today will become tomorrow's
distant memories.
You will overcome them,
and you will shine.
I am spellbound by the kindness in your eye.

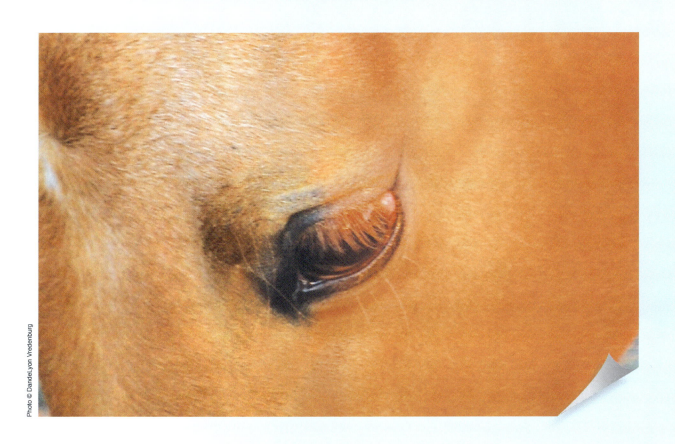

Gallop across the cold fields, feel the warmth from inside you, and
enjoy the bright sun on white snow.
We will travel close together, in rhythm, and with joy,
through all seasons, in sunlight and in shadow—
and we will outrun winter's chill.
When the weather turns from hot to cold, from rain to snow,
stay constant and true to those
you love and who love you.

Look beyond the mirror and see how beautiful you are,
in your kindness, compassion, and wisdom.
Know this: How you respond to the events in your life—not the events themselves—
become the forces that shape who you are and who you will become.
You have control of who you are—right here, right now,
for today, and for all of your tomorrows.
Your life belongs to you.
Live life to the fullest.

I will explore the world and be amazed at the joy that I find.
Yes. You are beautiful.
Yes. You have immense value.
Say it to yourself, and,
if your voice fails you, I will whisper it softly in your ear.
It's a whole new day. Even if yesterday didn't go so well,
put it behind you,
celebrate because you are special, and shine!
You deserve all that is wonderful in the world!

Celebrate the power of positive intention in your actions.
Be present in your now and live intently,
one moment at a time.
Find a quiet comfort in silence,
the kind that fills your ears with the perfect sound,
soothes your soul with a perfect peace, and
caresses you to your very core,
leaving you content and
unaware of your own breathing.
Shine On!

Freedom comes in many forms;
learn to recognize this fact and you will set yourself free.
I will forget, for a moment, the clutter of my everyday life.
I will find peace and solace in
the soft warmth of a horse's breath.
Celebrate the simple joys present in each day.
Those moments, connected,
make special memories.

I will stand quietly, in the sunlight,
and feel the warmth of kindness around me.
No matter how small or hard to find, it's there.
Let it make your day wonderful.
Let yourself shine!
Celebrate the simple joys of each day,
the ones without trumpets or spotlights
that you will remember
forever.

Freedom of your soul and spirit belongs to you.
Exercise it, allow it to shine,
and feel the joy that you bring to everyone around you.
Summon the courage to own yourself—who and what you are—
without apologies, excuses, or masks.
Share the real you with those you love and
experience magic of
true connections.

Make today a whole new world.
Forget about all the mistakes of yesterday and
celebrate the opportunities of this day.
Look around you and find something that you can laugh about.
In that instant, your day will be better.
Engage in today.
Cultivate that connection, encourage compassion, and stretch your courage.
Give yourself permission to shine brightly!

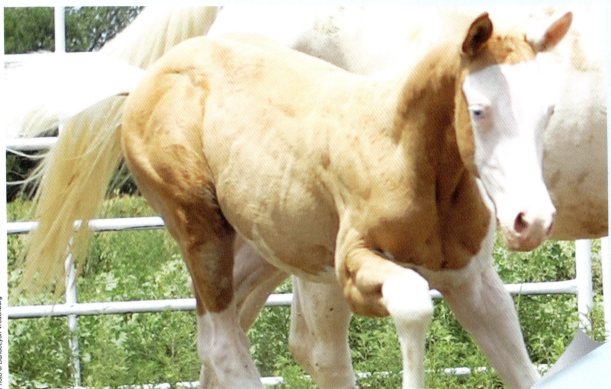

I will find moments of wonder and beauty in my day.
And I will remember them tomorrow.
I will shine!
Beauty is all around me.
I will look for it, see it, smile, and shine!
I will always be grateful for the mothers who have gone before me.
I honor their love, strength, and unending commitment.
Today, I will be grateful for the shelter of a mother's love.

Find the special moments in every day. They're there—
sometimes you just have to look closely to see them.
The perfectness of today is all around you,
in the softness of a horse's coat, a kind look from someone you love, or
the rhythm of a gentle breeze on your face.
Shine on!
In this quiet moment,
I know that you will always stand beside me and help me shine.
We sill shine together.

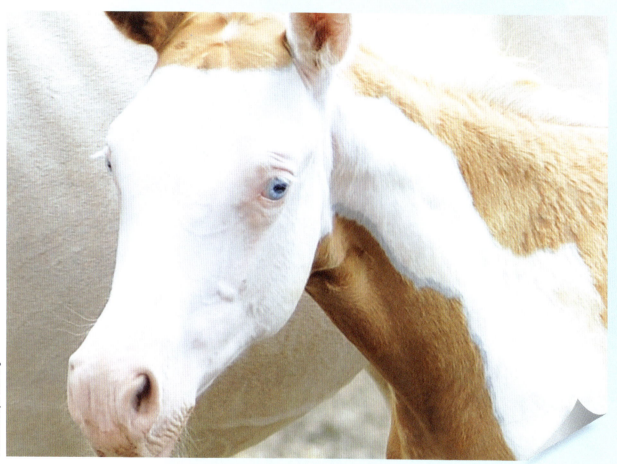

Today, take a minute to embrace yourself.
Celebrate your unique spirit!
There is only one of you, and you are radiant and rare.
We are so very different but we can share so much,
standing in the bright summer sunlight.
In the quiet graceful moments,
when I am most myself,
I feel the memories of pure connection that
I will always treasure.

Dance to your own tune! Prance at your own pace!
It's your life! Live it, love it,
and show the world how brightly
you shine!
Today, I will move forward with positive intention of action
in everything I do.
First, I will offer kindness to myself and then to those around me.
I will allow myself to shine.
And my world will shine with me.

I will grow strong, my legs will always carry me home,
and my heart will be full.
I will pin all my hopes on tomorrow,
but I will remember to make the most of today.
For every minute that I can, I will shine.
Stay close and true as you whisper softly to those you love.
Smile at the warmth of the sun and
the brightness of the stars,
and shine in all that you do.

Celebrate your life. It's spectacular—and so are you!
Every day is special...find the best in each moment of your life
and hold it close for all time.
We are always something more—never less—
after every experience in our beautifully shiny lives.
Today, be your own kind of beautiful.
Define yourself as you wish,
and share it with whom you choose.
We are all waiting for you to shine!

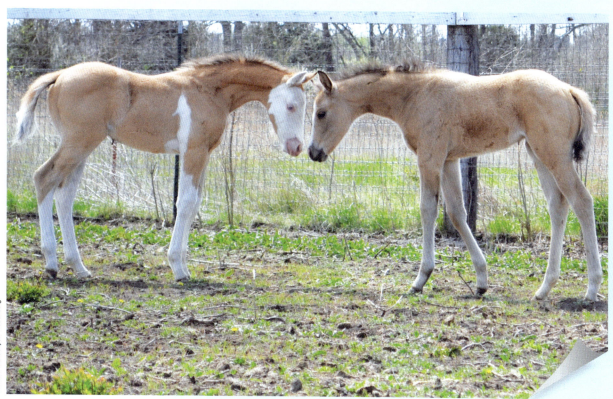

May your day be full of wonderful moments
that make great memories for tomorrow.
Live your life like you mean it. Because you do!
Grace is not always meek or gentle;
it is often strong and steady.
Let your grace—and your strength—shine.
I am grateful for the quiet days we spend together.
I will make the time to understand the importance of
these shiny moments of closeness.

That quiet voice, the one that gently guides you, is your instinct.

Learn to recognize it, honor it, and follow it.

I give thanks to the world's

artists, women, warriors, writers, mothers, sharers, and healers.

Life is messy, and life is beautiful.

Without the real truth,

all the bright paths and dark corners are lost.

I refuse to be mundane,

I refuse to be shamed,

and I refuse to be controlled.

Find the beauty that comes from knowing yourself
and exploring all that you are.
We all possess so many sides—
deciding which ones to nurture and strengthen becomes life's true adventure.
THIS day is YOURS.
If you are looking for a sign, THIS IS IT!
Love yourself, celebrate yourself, and know;
YOU are indeed a MIRACLE.
Today will be special.
I see it in your smile and feel it in my heart. Shine on.

Before the storm, feel the sunlight. Before the stillness,
play in a snow-covered field.
Before you sleep, remember all the beauty in your day...
and treasure it tomorrow. Shine on!
Say "YES" to all the great possibilities
that life has to offer.
Smile whenever you can,
laugh when the mood strikes you,
and shine in everything you do.

I am free. My soul and heart are mine to share,
not for the breaking or taking.
Today, my activities will honor my heart and soul.
Yes! No matter how busy I am,
I will make time to smile, and laugh, and play today.
I will shine!
Today I will take a moment to reflect and be grateful.
I will make choices that honor me.
I am deeply grateful for our soul connection.
Let's get shiny!

CPSIA information can be obtained
at www.ICGtesting.com
Printed in the USA
LVIC04n1825060814
397849LV00009B/176